The Catalog of Small Contentments

The Catalog of Small Contentments

Carolyn Martin

A Publication of The Poetry Box®

Editing & Book Design: Shawn Aveningo Sanders
Cover Design: Shawn Aveningo Sanders
Cover Photo: Samuel Austin
Author Photo: Robert R. Sanders

ISBN: 978-1-948461-85-6
Library of Congress Control Number: 2021935260
Printed in the United States of America.
Wholesale Distribution by Ingram.

Published by The Poetry Box ®, August 2021
   under The Poetry Box Select imprint
Portland, Oregon
ThePoetryBox.com

To those who are content to live their best today.

Health is the greatest gift,
contentment the greatest wealth,
faithfulness the best relationship.
—Buddha

~Contents~

Mandate

To those of you who will not die today:
walk through your home and bless the open doors,
the table set, the breadth of sun lounging
on the Persian rug. Catalog the small
contentments you have earned: eager words vying
for a poem, work you'll never have to do
again, backyard squirrels that entertain.
Praise every squill, crocus, and bleeding heart
that dares subvert winter's calendar.
Invite young mysteries in and seat them
between answers you have no questions for
and ponderables still unclassified.
It goes with saying: listen attentively.
Then tomorrow, if it arrives, repeat.

Breaking News: God's Rewilding Plan Leaked

According to a source high up and anonymous,
God will announce this week He's rewilding the earth.
He confesses He should have rested on day six
while He was on a cosmic roll, and laments
He missed the signs: bipeds, blinkered
by supremacy, would try to tame everything.

He admits to verte- and invertebrates
His human trial flopped. Therefore, next Sunday
pandas, peacocks, and silverbacks will play
in Times Square and caravans of antelope race
across Pennsylvania Avenue. Every boundary line,
dam, trellis, and mended wall will rumble down.
Steel, asphalt, and concrete will be banished heretofore.
So will summerizing gardens everywhere.

Believe what you like about our superiority,
God made a mistake. He should have advised
Adam and Eve *not* to procreate and lounged them
beneath the apple tree where they'd spend
their ten-score years in blissful innocence
rather than sweat through parental anxiety.

Between you and me, I'd support a God
as transparent as this. If His plan succeeds,
find me hanging out—waggishly naked
and wild—on the edge of some post-paradise
with monkeys, giraffes, dolphins,
elephants, koalas, and birds of every size.

Tethering

Be tethered to native pastures even if it reduces you
to a backyard in New York.
—Henry James

This morning's rain kept me inside and I swear
I heard the roses cheer and aggravated
crows crackle in the neighbor's cherry tree.

More natives to add to the menagerie
of feral cats, squirrels, birds, and moles
infiltrating too many poems.

My landscape is running out.
I may have to track down the Polish pasture
where my grandmother plowed courage and tears

and search out my Russian father's Manhattan flat.
If memory serves, it lacked a bathroom
and stove, not to mention hints of yard.

This morning's headlines might entice
with images of a Mars volcanic flow,
the *Deep Solar Minimum* of our quieting sun,

or the 17-year-locusts resurrecting again.
So much life happening beyond my sliding door
and the tethered views I bank my poems on.

And yet ... yesterday I watched errant robins ignore
worms to dine on suet cake, while my lone iris bulb—
its first time out—exploded into purple-black magnificence.

[. . .]

It's true I've yet to find words for how
a summer breeze trains lily leaves to wave at me
or why the brightest star in the western sky comforts my nights.

Always more, Nature whispers, from the corners of my yard.
Of course! I cheer, startling the song sparrow performing
her signature piece from the dripping apple tree.

Because the Sky

I enjoy the spring more than the autumn now.
One does, I think, as one gets older.
—Virginia Woolf, *Jacob's Room*

A brink-of-spring day and the sky invites
me to greet early robins fishing
for worms on my moss-soaked lawn.
She suggests I leave my camera behind.
Birds tend to bolt before I focus in.

But with eight decades in my rearview,
I'm not settling for repeated scenes.
I'm off to chase landscapes across state lines—
snapping photos of life sloughing off winter sleep.
I want to track Frost's return to his neighbor's budding wood
and find Wright's ponies munching twilight and grass.
Even Oliver's herons may find a moment
to stare and exchange curiosity.

What's unexplored is lost, I explain.
No offense to robins, worms, and moss.
There's more life beyond their well-groomed yard,
more answers to question before the spying
dark winds down my day.

The sky listens almost attentively
and, because she has better things to do,
gathers up her budding clouds, offers me
a shrug, moves on to the next neighborhood.

For Everything That Rises Must Converge

—Teilhard de Chardin, "Omega Point"

Sunrise and I'm about to murder
the crows congregated in our Douglas firs.

They're heckling sparrows pecking suet cake
dangling from a maple tree and can't conceive

these breakfasters should not be forced to rise
anywhere until they're satisfied.

I'm tempted to defy gravity and surf
the wind weaving through the evergreens.

From high above those nasty wings,
I'd warn them that my eye is on those sparrows

and other earth-bounded things.
With due respect, some must convene,

consort, converge before they're set to rise:
yeast and dough, soil and bulbs, flocks of geese.

Or, a weary soul like Virginia Woolf's,
slipping into a river's flow and waking—

to her surprise—on a wandering cyan gem
searching for eternal spring.

In Praise of Errancy

"This May Be the First Confirmed Errant Planet
Detected by Humans"
—Jesus Diaz, *Gizmodo*, 11/12/12

Jesus, how off track can you be?
What human arrogance to saddle
lonely CFBDSIR2149
with a name like *Melancholy*!

What's your gripe with an orphaned
cyan gem striking out on its own?
Of course it chose to drift
into emptiness. Why hang around
thirty bully stars in any galaxy?

There's nothing naughty in its quest.
Nothing delinquent in going rogue.
Bigger than four Jupiters,
it doesn't plan to mess with Earth.

Consider renaming it
Cosmic Adventurer or *Courageous Refugee.*
One-hundred light years away,
it's still conceiving an identity.

Old Age Ain't No Place for Sissies

—Bette Davis

We know our place. Any time
of day words stall between brain and tongue
and spelling turns into a phonics game.
We can't stop our skin from crinkling while we sleep
or knees from complaining they're abused.
Even when we squint, we confuse a pinecone for a bird.
Auditory skills? We've perfected, "Say again?"
Though earth quakes everywhere and sky glow
de-stars every city's nights, we've done well.
We've relegated drama to Hulu and Netflix
and made love visible to those with eyes to see.
We've lined up friends to scavenge through
our left-behinds before final trips to Goodwill.
For now we've earned old-age bravery by claiming
our place in the cosmic scheme. After intimate chats
with perennials, we're convinced death's impermanent.
Cheers to parades of sissies passing by.

To the Young Couple I Embarrassed on the Train
while Riding Home from the Airport
after a Trip to Rocky Mountain National Park

Blame my loose tongue on Rocky Mountain altitude
and the fact—indisputable at any height—
you were perfection across the aisle.
That's why my giddy self blurted out,
I wish I had a camera to catch
the profiles shifting in your seats
as you tracked freeway traffic bottling up.

I tried to apologize but that's not what I meant
at all. I wanted to say you were model-beautiful
and the way you leaned each into each was *love*
without words. Whatever stumbled out departed
at Powell Street where you left me your smiles—
embarrassed and amused.

If we had a longer ride, I would have told you
it's elk mating time and how Alpha bulls bugle
high-pitched challenges across meadows and hills.
I would have described the self-possessed cow
that brushed a pair of horns aside. She was having none of it.
I would have shared *tundra* is the Russian word
for *land without trees* and how I practiced
mindful breathing at 12,000 feet.

But time was what it was and you disembarked
before I could organize a travelog.
Someday, when you are holding hands downtown
and catch your reflections in a Starbucks window,

think about the woman who made you blush.
She wants you to know your portrait is cataloged
with mountains, glaciers, rivers, lakes,
and summer's last alpine blooms: the ones
with yellow petals holding on wildly to golden hearts.

Across Nine Zones: From Oregon to South Africa

While I sleep and dream of nothing memorable,
the customer care rep sits at his home office desk
redressing Amazon's complaints. By the time
my coffee's brewed, I fantasize
he's assuaged the irate Dublin lass who hates
her red lip gloss. (Not the color advertised.)
To her surprise, he tells her keep the tube—
a friend might love its cherry/berry/wine—
and expect a full refund by noon.
He's also emailed labels for returns:
the faulty Instant Pot® in Portugal,
a "Tempt Me Woman" swimsuit in Brazil,
Oneida Flatware—16-piece—in Maine.

He's dreaming about his end-of-day
when I call him eight a.m. my time
about deliveries delayed.
He describes in English, polished and precise,
a factory flood somewhere. That satisfies
and so does the news he's in South Africa.
I want to know his season of year.
Does he garden or hike?
His favorite book? TV show?
What it's like to spend the day with people everywhere?

Flush with pleasantries, he catches me off guard.
I'm your future, you're my past.
With our *present* nine time zones apart, it takes me
time to feel his drift and join his laugh.

I suggest we check with Einstein—maybe Plato,
Augustine, and Kant—to see if they agree.

Before we disconnect, he promises
should he suspect the world is spinning toward its end,
he'll alert me via my current email address
before doom reaches Oregon.

Marx Was Right

History repeats itself
as *tragedy*,
then settles
into *farce*.
And so was Joyce
slogging through
his own *nightmare,*
and Napoleon
battling
a *fable agreed upon.*
Which leads me
to conclude
the last human sound
before the galaxy
consumes itself
won't be a whimper
or a scream.
Rather, gasping stars
will hear
our groans.
Self-important
as we think we are,
we'll grasp that life
was a fidgety dream
fabulists devised
to entertain our sleep.

Hypnopedia

When you can lounge in a corner
of your dreams—sipping lattes
or slugging whiskey neat—who needs
syllabi, seminars, or student debt?

Snooze while Shakespeare scratches out
soliloquies and Hannibal his battle plans.
Catalog the universe across your sheets
with Hawkins and Einstein, then race

a bike or hybrid car around your quilt
and track the myths of origins.
Delight in mysteries of who created
whom/where/how/why/when.

If a garbage truck should drown out
Darwin's speech or a nagging crow disturb
your dig-down-deep into the earth,
pull a feathered pillow over your head.

Put your dreams on pause and focus on
your breath. Then, as quiet settles in,
invite them back to their current course.
There's more to learn before the next bell rings.

Reading Billy Collins at 2 A.M.

It might have been the hunter's moon sneaking
through the shades or anxiety for kittens freezing
in our yard. No matter, it's sleep *interruptus* again.

What absurdity to click my MacBook on and bypass
Hulu and Netflix to read his poetry when it's predictable:
on any given day it only takes three to rev me up.

Why should now be different? Sleeplessness is night school
in disguise so, here in the classroom of tangled sheets,
I follow the cadence of his voice, sussing out

a mind that floats and twists, scribbling notes
by computer light. If my jottings are legible,
tomorrow I'll draft a poem to tussle with.

At 3:05: surrender to a pill, unconcerned I'll fall
into a dream about apples in New England
or embroidered cloths in Ireland. No, I'll stroll

Parisian streets chatting with the poet about
why he thinks poems hold the history of the human heart
and why his never end the way I expect.

We'll head for the restaurant where a collie of a certain age
waits at a table set for three. By the time we arrive,
she has sampled the biscuits *du jour* and ordered us a tray.

The waiter guides us to our seats and hands the wine list
to the golden dog who, with her elegant sixth sense,
knows "The Day Lassie Died" has popped into my head.

Passing me a smile, she asks the waiter how he rates
Chateau Margaux Pavillon Rouge. The poet scribbles
furiously in a notepad propped on his salad plate.

Resiliency

The wastepaper basket is the writer's best friend.
                    —Isaac Bashevis Singer

Scribbled on bank slips, grocery receipts,
and note pads from a dozen charities,
snips of words hide in dismissive dark.
Until, that is, they're dumped into recycling
and escape with an errant breeze
prancing around the neighborhood.

A divorcee walking her Cavachon
picks up—uncrumpled and intact—
I thought of you today/but can't remember why.
She laughs to herself—her pet annoyed
by the sudden pause—*How about
a hundred whys I never think?*
Proud of her resiliency, she tucks the lines
into a neighbor's cedar fence.

Farther down the street, a therapist—
out to free his mind before his office turns
off birdsongs and wafts of wisteria—
grabs a scrap and frowns. *Most things I say/
aren't worth the air I breathe.*
Depression, he suspects as he jogs in place,
memorizing words for tomorrow's consult team.

With morning on the run,
the world is shutting down lands

on a dandelioned lawn with *everything*
that rises must—impatient for an audience.
While *I want to tell the truth/*
and already said too much
catches its breath beneath a flowering plum.
Proud of its profundity, it questions
why it's lying here and not in the first
or last lines of a prize-winning poem.

Contemplating Distancing

I want to tell the truth
and already said too much
but what if I am the distance from myself?

~

In Costco and Home Depot parking lots,
I rip off my homemade mask and breathe.
Oh, the fresh gift of air after stale breath recycling!

~

The TED Talk I would give if someone asked:
"How to Live a Boring Life with Graceful Elegance."

~

What I no longer need: a calendar,
a full tank of gas, lipstick, an excuse to nap.

~

Things I saw once and will always see:
The grease stain on my new T-shirt
The cobweb swaying on the chandelier
The light vacating dying eyes

~

When TV bores and my eyes can't grasp
another paragraph, I clean the house
beyond reasoning.

❧

Nature multi-tasks all the time,
but not my nature or my time.

❧

Most things I say aren't worth white space
or oxygen. Somewhere someone is doing
what I want to do better than I can.

❧

A distancing haiku:

>   raindrops in the curl
>   of a ginkgo leaf
>   quarantine

❧

Let creative plagues be on my house—like the ones
that conceived Newton's calculus and gravity
and Shakespeare's Macbeth, Lear, and Anthony.

Rules of Haiku

In every classroom in America
they're counting out 5-7-5
with as much certainty
as Columbus sailed the ocean blue
and Des Moines is the capital of Iowa.

Teachers seem pleased
their kids recognize syllables—
a skill useful for songsters, poets,
and typographers in any state
with blue waters or cornfields.

Meanwhile,
under the spreading chestnut tree
outside PS 105, Issa is chortling
as Bashō shapes a frown.

What fun! the younger grins.
They're playing at our poetry.

Never works, the elder says,
sipping Moroccan Mint.
They overdo syllables.

Suddenly,
Mrs. Teacher-of-the-Month
aims for the fourth-grade hand
pointing at the curious ant
stalled on a computer screen.

It's stopped to ponder the haiku-of-the day—
adding wings
to the red pepper
a dragonfly—
The three stare confused.

What do dragonflies have to do
with red peppers in twelve syllables?

Don't Follow a Good Dead Poet,
but Search for What He Searched for

—Bashō

Well said, Matsuo.
I like this sentence a lot.
I liked it even more
when Wikipedia said
you re-named yourself *Tosei*—
"unripe peach in blue"—
before you settled down
to life as *Bashō*,
the "banana tree."

I could stop right here
since we both agree
mimicking poets,
alive or deceased,
is easier than figuring out
the *perhaps/maybe/*
of course/that's it of what
they were searching for.

But then again,
it all comes down to
Truth/Beauty/Love/
Suffering/Death/Seize the Day.
What's left?

Perhaps you could
comment on
my new haiku:

winter thaw
sounds of sun
on snow

Following or searching for?

About Nothing

This morning nothing's on my mind but feeding
backyard birds and tracking the light frost lounging
on the neighbors' roofs. The sun is on tour
through Douglas firs and I'm curious about melting time.

Then it occurred I should pencil in slogging
through the grass to chide the moss winter didn't kill
and praise bleeding hearts' return. And what a mistake
to miss the star magnolia tree. Its pussy willows
bloom before they turn to leaves.

I should contemplate the confused cactus
in the family room announcing Christmas
in early spring. Followed by closets needing breathing space
and bookshelves begging for relief from never-reads.
Of course, I could catalog every wall
and re-evaluate excessive steel-cut art,
photographs, ceramic plaques designed to motivate.
A favorite? *What can you afford to live without?*

I'd love to grab a pen and explore
Buddha's claim contentment is the greatest wealth,
but a sparrow is peeking through the sliding door.
Her hungry eyes complain I forgot
what I woke this morning for. *Nothing
isn't nourishing,* she bobs her head. Agreed.

A Sonnet for Early Spring

When April mixes memory and moss,
twenty moles pilgrimage the yard and toss
aerated soil around our flower beds.
When three feral cats train to track red-heads
and orange-tails, there—beneath crusty leaves—
baby snails, grubs, and worms yearn to believe
the world was made for them. When daylight frees
itself from thoughts of winter-death and trees
convince the earth oblivion's a hoax,
then every squill and bee engenders hope
that sundry folk, daffodils, and sweet peas
will raise voices with saints of every creed.
They'll inspire young bleeding hearts to sing
about the lean elegance of waking spring.

Pay Attention and You're Saved

It pays to pay attention—which is not
like paying bills, the pizza delivery guy,
or the piper—wherever he may pipe.

Nor is it like paying compliments,
taxes, penalties, dues, visits, respect,
or up-down-forward-back for anything.

Crime doesn't pay, unless it does.
Neither does arrogance when you nip
your own line to title a poem.

But when oblivion's about to hit
pay dirt and saving's worth the fight,
rouse attention, slumped in the doorway

of your shuttered mind. Focus its eyes
on barefaced possibilities peeking
through blossoms of an aging cherry tree.

Dear Type-A Friend,

This is to let you know I'm newly funemployed.
I've grown weary of the restless noise
of earth, so I plan to gadabout the universe
in search of alternatives to humanoids.
Perhaps I'll terraform an asteroid
and confirm the latest scientific claims
it contains quintillions in gold.
I'll appoint myself its CEO
and send you a prospectus once
I've penciled out investment strategies.
In the meantime, feel free to take
treasures from my condo.
The Hunan prints might intrigue,
as well as the Queen Anne dining set,
shelves of eclectic books,
and perennials potted on the patio.
Set my telescope in your backyard and aim
it toward the space between Jupiter and Mars.
You may see my new digs weaving
through the star-clogged sky.
If I find the time, I'll wave.

To My About-to-Be-Ex Therapist

About our session this afternoon, I'm confused:
you diagnosed my ergophobia with sadness
in your voice. No offense, but after 40 years
of Type-A overdrive, I've earned this new paradigm.
Put this in your notes: I've replaced chronic threats
of nothing-to-do with perfected laziness.
My fear of boredom? Relieved by mindfulness.
From my ergonomic chair, I spend hours
tracing the texture of walls and studying
slight tilts of Chinese serigraphs.
I'm happy to report the woman side-saddling
the panther's back hasn't slipped off yet
and the lotus pond hasn't flooded our family room.
As for the cobwebs swaying behind the étagère?
They haven't ceased to captivate. Anyway,
thanks for helping me define work as what
I say it is. My business suits and black pumps
are up for grabs at Goodwill; my office files
free of contracts, flight plans, and syllabi.
I'm noodling with a blog about the joys
of nothing much. Maybe you'll subscribe.

Superannuation

Mornings roll out the same—street lights snap
off, solars sip sun, cars roar to work.
But, severed from my job, I'm confused.

My trashcan sits un-emptied on the curb.
Yesterday I missed Macy's on line sale
and every day my do-nothing list expands.

Desperate, I've started to converse
with the antic ant pacing on my TV tray.
This morning she complains my Sharpies

are scattered like reckless beached logs.
They're drying out, she says,
and I'm so beyond your adult coloring.

She's climbed the books, she claims,
balanced near my coffee cup and applauds
Bel Canto and *The Rain in Portugal.*

She's also critiqued scribbled lines
of poetry I drop on the floor.
She's not enamored, she says,

with *the lean elegance of choice,*
but *What if oblivion is a hoax?*
gives her pause. Her advice?

I should become more astonishing.
That gives me pause.
The late blooms in my yard—asters,

mums, dipladenia—she points out,
thirst for a literary home.
The feral cat lolling in the sun?

He'd love an update of *Split the lark.*
And the squirrel on the side yard fence ...
I stop her in her tracks.

Michael Crichton's *Prey* just jogged
across my mind. What if nanotechnology
could shrink me below her size?

I roll out this idea and, pacing back and forth,
she admits it would refine our relationship.
She assigns me a fixed due date.

Time Management in Grand Central Bakery

On a morning when summer can't decide
whether to go or stay, couples drape
over benches outside and moms with kids
line up inside before the pastry case.
Muffins, jammers, scones? They can't agree.

A friend and I sip lattes and play
at catching up. With delight, she hands me
her key to productive retirement: days
carved into thirty-minute increments.
Morning meditation to a bedside book,
she ticks off her life—practical, precise.
That's it, she smiles a knowing smile,
convinced I'll agree.

How to admit I'm enamored
with time's messiness? I check email
fifty times a day, Facebook
and Submittable about the same.
My breed of discipline is untamed
and goals and lists smack of vanity.
After thirteen retired years, I dwell in spots
of time where I play unscripted dramas out.

But I assure my friend efficiency gurus
would approve her strategy, and just in time—
over pecan rolls and coffees-of-the-day—
a barista rings a saving bell.
My "Make Your Own Sandwich" is up.

Twenty-One Epigraphs for Poems
Celebrating the Retirement of Work Addicts

Only disconnect.

Slow down aggressively.

Do nothing and rest afterwards.

Sit, stare, and move the wall.

You have the right to remain silent.

Nothing-happening is not a threat.

Revel in redundancy.

Put all your goals in a box and burn that box.

Love to do what's now.

A quiet mind hears the soul.

Embrace the lean elegance of choice.

Trick yourself into happiness.

Cultivate primordial confidence.

Bask in the groundless paradox of ambiguity.

[. . .]

Ponder: Where does "it" take "time"?

Be proud of your humility.

Celebrate a chasm's closing.

Peel off the remnants of demands.

Nothing is ever as good or as bad as you anticipate.

Truth will find you and make you beautiful.

Stand outside yourself and record the ecstasy.

This Morning's Obituaries

My second slice of toast and Monday's score:
Seven men, three women, one boy:
93 to 13 in favor of no one.

Not the Judge, mechanic, Ph.D.,
teacher, wrestler, trucker, or auctioneer.
Not the three grandmothers who cared
for husbands and wayward kids.
Certainly not the bright-smile lad skidding
off a go-cart track near the finish line.

With 93 there's reason, 73 might make sense,
but 13's an atrocity. I pray those men
will take the boy aside and teach him
how to wrestle with challenges
shortened lives don't have the time to face:
how to balance scales and rev engines up;
how to fend off fast-flung words in parking lots;
how to fill black holes and shatter meteors.

I pray those grandmothers claim him
as their own and teach him how to bake
and sew, how to make flowers smile,
how giving and receiving are the same.

Breaking bread, I bless them all and hope
they've settled in the same neighborhood:
the one where errant angels race around
the go-cart track a few clouds away
from freshly painted mansions
and the Grand Central Bakery.

Music to Disappear By

The melody? It's never recognizable,
the harpist says. Eyes closed, her fingers pluck
in sync with my father's dying breaths.

I sit by his side, mesmerized by their duet.
He, the ancient wind; she, an Aeolian
composing his life in tranquil tones.

He'd be amused if he could hear himself
dictating notes beneath sharp-cornered sheets—
this maestro of baseball games, lawnmowers,

corny jokes. This low-keyed man who loathed
his paper-pushing job, could lose himself
in our backyard, called me his poet champ.

Here, now—sirens, horns, quibblings on the street
mute themselves. Hallway voices pause,
awed by vibrations wafting through

the hospice door. My father's eyes find mine
and, through a fading stare, ask me to record
his melody before it disappears.

What the Recently Dead Are Doing

While the living are busy collecting sympathy
    and casseroles—before confronting closets
        and unpaid bills, after contacting Social Security,
            insurance, and far-flung relatives—

the just-dead dead are roaming through
    clouded neighborhoods puzzled by empty lots
        where their self-styled mansions should be.
            They double-check addresses, review promises.

Someone got something wrong.

At the end of one leaf-less street, a school
    of dim-haloed wings are bantering with Plato,
        Darwin, Shakespeare, Marx, and Frost
            about the myths of Heaven and eternity.

Someone proposed good stories keep the good in tow.

But the eavesdropping dead complain, *We paid
    our dues for everlasting bliss. We're owed.*
        Wings droop. Thinkers roll their eyes.
            The evening breeze does what breezes do.

Someone flips the bardo's hourglass.

Meanwhile, my father lies in a casket in Florida.
    He forgot to turn the sprinklers off and take the garbage out,
        forgot to hang the bronze sun-burst on the backyard fence,
            forgot to tell my mother/his best friend he loved her first.

[. . .]

He tells passers-by he has work to do and almost rises
from his satin sheets when he recalls—with twinges
of relief—Death is a transient stopping by
from time to time to pack up memories.

Someone tallies grains of sand and calls it a day.

After Reading Khaled Hosseini's *Sea Prayer*

Before I could read
or knew the word *refugee*,
my Russian father tossed me
into waves along the Jersey shore.
Safe in his sight, I learned
to navigate—over, under, with.
No need to pray to any god.

Here, now—miles of time away
from sand and waves and my father's eyes—
Hosseini's not-for-children children's book:

On Syria's sea edge,
a father holds his son.
Rumors of wild flowers,
olive trees, goats and cows,
market smells, a thousand
boyhood dreams drown
in city ruins where craters
masquerade as swimming pools
and believers and non-
share slits of sun slipping
through bricks and beams.

Dogs are feral now
and Death sleeps in every house
in every room and I can barely
bear to read the father's prayer.
All he asks? When land slips
away and their boat heaves

[. . .]

and tilts, safety for his child.
A simple parent's simple plea:
safe passage for his son.

But, I want to scream,
what's this praying worth?
When indifferent gods have failed
to guide ten thousand souls
across indifferent seas,
what is praying worth?

I snap the book shut and conjure up
my dad. We grab our bathing suits
and crash through resistant waves.
We're bound to save one determined boat
from an unwelcoming sea.

In the Doctor's Waiting Room

No one's here on this snowy afternoon
but an old guy contemplating *Field and Stream,*
a Christmas cactus past its prime, and me.

How beautiful outside! I break silence as I tend to do
when connections seem makeable and time agrees
to hurry by if conversation clears the way.

The cactus already knows and the flannel shirt frowns
at this smallest of talk. *Got me,* he says, staring
beyond his boots. *Can't see beauty anywhere.*

I restrain a reply and wait him out: One son dead.
One daughter dead. One wife of forty years lost
in memory care. Some days she remembers him.

Why, he almost cries, *does God punish me?*
"Dark night of the soul" races across my mind
and I'm tempted to insist God is merciful.

But where's the good in flip theology?
I've seen grief before. Held it in my arms,
stroked its head resting on my lap. I've walked

it up and down city streets, listening to
its sad/angry/guilty words. Stood guard
at gravesides as it crumbled to the ground.

From what I've learned of betrayal and hurt,
cruelty and loss, there is no grief
like ours and earth is rich with it.

He pours his out over a magazine.
The cactus bows. Comfort—fragile and rare—
hides out alone. I hold my tongue.

Hollow

A mother never loses loss:
my mantra since our baby died.
My husband cannot hear the screams
I bury in the basement walls
or divine what my half-smiles mean.
Four years...he's numb to my despair.
I despise the peace he has become.

We take our boy's ashes everywhere—
his sisters are convinced he wants to go.
They travel-sticker every inch of cherry wood
and entertain with how they rescued turtle eggs
hatching in Los Cabos sun and cheered the ape
rocking her newborn in San Diego's zoo.
How they giggled at male elk bugling for mates
across a Rocky Mountain field and fed
fistfuls of hay to nudging goats at 4-H.
Seven and three, they talk to him as much as they talk to me.

Two girls, one boy, I always say.
When strangers—like the woman on the plane
or the couple moving in next door—seem confused
seeing only two, I seize the opening:
Two years old. In our arms. In our bed.
If curiosity invites, I explain his rare disease
and how we prayed to keep him warm.
What I won't admit: I lock my bedroom door
and trace his outline on our sheets
a dozen times a day.

A Week Late

Crystal Springs Rhododendron Garden
Portland, Oregon

Rhododendrons droop above spent azaleas and third graders—
field-tripping with their pads and #2s—don't care. They've come
to draw what's left: waterfalls, irises, dogwood, fern, herons,
mallards, geese. *We can't talk to strangers*, pigtails rebuff my
praise of her woodland scene. A mother-chaperone—over-
weary in the post-noon sun—nods a smile. Some lessons take.
Suddenly a flock of roaming kids shouts us toward the lake's far
edge where goslings congregate—unaware their yellow fluff will
soon decorate a classroom wall and enchant 200 friends on my
Facebook page.

Anatidaephobia

On the far side
of the lake,
they're calculating
how to shake me
from my bench
so I'll leave
my lunch behind.

Despicable—these
ducks who seem
innocent enough,
yet
trouble waterways
to ruffle me
with unrelenting eyes.

I admit
every staring thing
unhinges me:
the maple peering
into our living room,
the sparrow spying
on the patio,
the kid pounding
on his steering wheel
as I stroll within
crosswalk lines.
Nothing, it seems,
respects
the grace of privacy.

Despite
psychologists' protests,
this phobia is real—
as real as
Thinking makes it so.

Tomorrow
I'll tackle
exposure therapy
and face off
every anatidae
in town.

For now,
deep breaths
summon up a prayer
that dabblers, divers,
and buffleheads
will close their eyes
once they realize
all I have is hummus
spread edge-to-edge
on organic celery.

Mosaic of a Spring Day in Quarantine

From the mauve armchair in my living room:
a flowering pink quince hosts a hummingbird.
Urgent leaves evict white blooms from the magnolia tree.
A maple's tight-fisted reds blur the truck
marked Prime, crawling around a UPS delivery.

This: a spot of time witnessed from a space
I rarely occupy. That's it.

And yet, for no other reason than to keep
me in my seat, the hero in the novel I was reading
last night before I remembered sleep
jogs up our cul-de-sac.

A mortician in this murder mystery,
he claims people trapped in doomed airplanes
may yearn to leave behind notes of love or regret.
How? Swallow them.
The stomach saves, he maintains and pulls
indicting words from a woman's cavity.

Worth a morning's wait.
How else would I know the neighbor
to the south is getting a new flat screen;
the one to the north, a box from Vitacost?
How else would I learn that words
—consumed and absorbed—survive?

From Your Resident Steller's Jay

Let's be clear: you are not my favorite.
The way you prance around the yard elated
that your slug bait worked rattles
me and makes me want to squawk.

And so does the wimpy bush
that used to be a sugar maple tree
and the fountain you turned into a flower pot.
What's your gripe with shade and water falls?

You've been hoodwinked to believe
I bully sparrows dining on suet cake.
The fact? I'm loosening that hunk of lard
so little beaks don't strain so much.

As for the raccoons tearing up your lawn:
you never applaud my pre-dawn raids
where I save five dozen grateful grubs
cowering in your mossy grass.

In spite of … something about you attracts.
Maybe it's how you cite me in your poems
although you cannot spell my name.
I'm a *Steller's* not a *stellar* jay.

Please correct and then revise the one
about the feral cat that watches me nip nuts
from a clueless squirrel. You sit her on a *catbird seat*:
a prejudicial term implying feline superiority.

One more thing: consider a new birdfeeder.
The tinny one at the backyard fence sways
and my wings fatigue when I try to peck
sunflower seeds from multi-grains. By the way,

good choice: Audubon's a top-shelf brand.
Ten-pound sacks are on sale at Backyard Birds
along with the Squirrel-Be-Gone Country House
and the Perky-Pet Deluxe Chalet

In Production: *The Flamboyance of Flamingoes*

Today the Bolshoi Ballet proudly announced
their world-renowned company of swans will play
the lead in this new ornithologic musical.

A paddle of ducks from Des Moines are lined up
as understudies and a waddle of penguins
from the San Diego Zoo as the chorus line.

Set in New York, this classic dramedy
tracks a congress of crows as it uncovers
a raven conspiracy to kidnap ugly ducklings

and deliver them to a kettle of hawks
terrorizing Central Park. In a pivotal scene—
a party set in a posh high rise—

socialites are flamingoes in disguise
and looming owls spy from the balcony.
Script writers are hiding major plot twists

in the wings. It's anybody's guess why
piteous doves fly through every scene
and penguins, in a tour de force, sing off key.

Playing Second Violin

It's none of my business but sitting near
the first violin, I can feel the confidence
that never fails a Mozart score and the appeal
of her swaying arms, shoulders, and hair
to the maestro who bows through applause,
turns to shake her hand, and asks her out for drinks
before the first French horn begins his climb
over flutes, oboes, and clarinets
to offer her the same, but she's packed her bow
and Master Linn for an evening out beyond
the pit so, when he arrives at her empty seat—
his brass muted with regret and defeat—
he rushes by without a glance and ignores
my *sotto voce* hum of *I've been here before.*

Private Libraries

Downton Abbey to Oregon

What luxury! One room designed for walls
of words, a well-banked fireplace, a bell
at royal fingertips to announce they require
tea or an escort to invite over-staying guests
off the premises. Evening cigars,
brandy snifters, land-management arguments.

Decades away, I'm unashamed to boast
my taupe salt box spills scripts into every space.
Fiction fills the living room; the bedroom, autobiography.
The kitchen—where I write more than cook—piles of poetry.
The foyer's crystal chandelier contains the history of design;
the office, inventions like the dimmer switch.

And there's a mystery section in our backyard.
Snapdragons and mums disguise themselves
as perennials, and feral kittens—one black, one white—
leave us clueless about paternity.

After cataloging books, I flip on my gas fireplace
and welcome Dame Maggie Smith for tea. We reminisce
about her Jean Brody prime and how she rocked
the stage with *Kiss me quick before my body rots*
in *Private Lives*. That, before she mastered wizardry
and Violet's sharp-tongued wit.

She's about to list her favorite royal jibes
when an oven's ding—audible beneath a swirling
Turner sky—announces dinner's ready to be served
in the room filled with culinary history.

It Was a Dark and Rainy Night
at the Poetry Salon

where the featured reader, enamored with smiles
and polite applause, forgets to take a break.
When he says, *Three or four more*, I'm undone.

Off the sofa, over stretched-out legs,
passed glasses of wine caressed attentively
in hands craftier than mine, I find the bathroom

unoccupied—except for a slow drip in the sink
and a basket full of magazines. I could be content
to spend the night in this retreat, muting the *ahs*

from the living room, tamping the groans of windows
shivering from the rain. Here: submission calls,
elegies for Broadway shows, photos of expiring worlds,

and, to my surprise, memories of a teenage girl
hiding in the tub with *For Whom the Bell Tolls*.
Entrenched in love scenes, she ignores candles

dripping down her birthday cake and giggles
from a party game. *A waste*, she looks at me,
this sweet sixteen surprise. Why...but a determined rap

on the door announces a line flooding the hall.
The girl commiserates. This, before I can ask
if she's heard of Ann Patchett and *Bel Canto*.

Partners of Poets Anonymous (POPA)
Opening for Business

We are pleased to announce
we are getting organized even as they type.

Our name—alliterative with a snappy acronym—
has been approved along with our statement of intent:

*We support those who appear—favorably
or not—in their partner's poetry.*

We agree even when references are compliments,
they prompt a blushing slump in front row seats

while our partners steal the stage and earn
applauds—and often laughs—at our expense.

On first Mondays, we'll gather to commiserate—
in spite of the odds it's some poet's birthday—

and rotate through bookstores, libraries,
coffee shops, or any other site where poets read.

We want our hosts to understand how it feels
to lie naked on a page—even quasi-anonymously.

At our kick-off event, we'll hash out
By-Laws, elect a board, and discuss raising funds.

Monies will be earmarked for annual retreats
as far away as possible from poets sitting

[. . .]

alone in restaurants, softening their eyes
surreptitiously across a glass of wine—

waiting, no doubt, to scribble everything
we do or say in a treacherous notebook.

A caveat: If one day we discover we miss
our smile, eyes, shoulders, turn of head, or timbre

of voice landing in the monument of a poem;
or if we say something no one else could say

and find it abandoned on some wordless road;
or if we start to grieve for those sweet renderings

of who we are in well-crafted verse—if that day
arrives, we'll disband and burn our By-Laws.

To You, My Dear First Reader

Perhaps you were distracted. Before you scanned
my newest poem, I heard your cell phone ping
and the neighbors let loose another string of obscenities.

In any event, you didn't seem to mind my lack of reference
to how you roll your eyes when I say stupid stuff
or how you know more than me about almost everything.

Did you notice I avoided feral cats? They may be
over-done—like Oliver's herons or the walks
Collins takes while scouting for a poem.

I felt your almost-smile at my natural touch:
the ranting Steller's jays and the marching sugar ants.
Anyway, how about I read this draft out loud?

Your musician's ear would spot internal rhymes
as well as the *soto voce* in the penultimate line.
That doesn't appeal? One read-through was enough?

Of course, you can answer your texts and turn the TV on.
I'd recommend the first season of *Perfect Harmony* on Hulu
and the sixth of *Schitt's Creek* on Netflix.

Just Saying

This morning
you never stopped.
Of course
I wanted to hear
every detail about
yesterday's barbeque
in your old neighborhood
and who married whom
and the history of their kids
and how your childhood tribe
crept across
the grouchy neighbor's yard
on sulky summer nights.

I was also intrigued
by the Kennedy conspiracy,
how magnesium
is essential for the brain,
and why I should avoid
every wheat-filled thing.

I almost snuck in
Thích Nhất Hạnh's
The bread we eat is the whole cosmos,
but his words got lost
in the orbit of your voice
along with gardenia blooms,
my latest poem,
and the stream of clouds
easing from the coast.

In case you're interested,
I've bookmarked these
along with the truth
that announced itself
in a waking dream:
we are magnetized
steadily.

Meet me for a chat
on the patio tonight.
Perhaps you'll acquiesce
when I quote John Donne:
*For God sake hold
your tongue and let me love.*

Blamestorming

...never blame the lettuce.
—Thích Nhất Hạnh

Must be
the slugs
munching
to the music
of the night
or the clogged
soaker hose
or malicious
hailstorms
barnstorming
the yard.

Must be
the timbre
of your voice
that rolls my eyes
when you guarantee
wilted greens
are my mistake
like
every perfect storm
smashing
our serenity.

Must be
some ancient god
who dabbled
in DNA
so humanoids
would blame
every offense
on mothers
lovers
friends and
primal innocence.

Andragogy 101

Dear Adult Learner,

Welcome to "How to Live a Mature Life
with Autonomy." For our first class,
bring a detailed list of your major mistakes
from the time you were six—particularly
the ones still burning in your gut.
They will form our syllabus.

We'll excavate each gaffe for the lessons
they provide and problem-solve how
to re-frame your life with time-tested strategies.
We'll mitigate the past and lighten up today.
Which path you choose is up to you.

The requirements for a passing grade?
Apply what you learn immediately.
Your spouse (current or ex-), kids, boss,
neighbors, friends, and near-by relatives
will be asked to submit a final report
confirming your complicity. In two weeks
I expect a comprehensive contact list.

One caveat: if your motivation to learn
is not internalized or, if you're still dipping
your feet in the childhood swamp of blame,
revisit this semester's catalog.
There are dozens of offerings that might be
better fits. Transfer into one today.

With Apologies to Mary Oliver

(1935-2019)

My letter would have been
polite and inquisitive
about the herons
gliding
through your poetry.
I wanted to know
how many times
the same gangly bird
could invade
the same landscape.
I would have asked
if you knew about
Mozart's too-many-notes—
a critique
within high praise.
Astute enough,
you'd get the point.
But you died.
I'd be remiss
not to admit
my feral cats
equal your birds—
along with fixations
on Billy Collins,
haiku, and the *Word
of the Day.*

Dear Billy Collins,

If I told you I have six collections of my own,
you would politely nod and act impressed—
you with your fifteen, walls of awards,
and videos on well-lit platforms
where you never need to adjust the mic
because its height is designed for you—
as is the lectern and semi-comfortable chair
where you sit with a practiced host
who asks questions I've memorized the answers to.

That's because I've tracked your You-Tube clips
repeatedly for insights, inspirations, or—
if Truth nudges me hard enough—excuses
to avoid Googling great cities of the world
for images to upscale a mediocre poem
that refuses to say where it wants to go.

You, on the other hand, never fail to disappoint—
like the feral cat who strolls across
the patio and swats the sliding door
or the flicker who delights in my suet cake.

I count on certain things: that noncommittal pet,
an orange feather lying in the grass, and your glasses
that may—or not—stay on your nose
while you read from *The Rain in Portugal*
or from *Sailing Alone Around a Room*—
a nautical activity, I'm not ashamed
to admit, I practice when no one's home.

The Best of 42 Writers' Rules for Writing

Have regrets. They are fuel.
The first 12 years are the worst.

Laugh at your own jokes.
You're a Genius all the time.

Beware of tidiness.
Visionary tics shiver in the chest.

Never ride a bike with the brakes on.
Be a crazy dumb saint of the mind.

Stay in your mental pajamas all day.
Do back exercises. Pain is distracting.

Cement a little every day, rather than add new fertilizers.
Leave out the parts readers tend to skip.

Take no notice of anyone you don't respect.
You can also do all that with whiskey.

Read Keats's letters.
Honor the miraculousness of the ordinary.

Write without pay until somebody offers pay.
Cheer up by reading biographies of writers who went insane.

Perfection is like chasing the horizon.
Prayer might work.

Don't be a draught-horse!
... you chose it, so don't whine.

Take a pencil to write with on airplanes.
You see more sitting still than chasing after.

Remember there is no such thing as nonsense.
Good ideas are often murdered by better ones.

Never complain of being misunderstood.
Have humility.

If the rhythm of your prose is broken, read poetry.
Have more humility.

Don't drink and write at the same time.
Bad writing is contagious.

Your audience is one single reader.
Avoid cliques, gangs, groups.

Writing is work. It's also gambling.
Do feel anxiety—it's the job.

In Praise of Community

—with thanks to Merriam-Webster Online

A coterie of chick-a-dees
communes
in my maple tree.
A tribe of constellations
self-distances
in a nightfall sky.
Brown-robed monastics
bow
before broken bread.
Circles of poets
zoom
from their inspiration rooms.
Fellowships of love
connect
black/brown/yellow/white/red.

Let's praise
every synonym
that binds, bonds, ties, unites
and make a communal vow:
if any family, circle,
troop, guild, league,
club, or neighborhood
morphs
into a clique, sect, gang,
faction, or closed shop,
we'll revise
our acclaim and delete

our membership
without
a moment's doubt.

Summer Afternoon

... to me those have always been the two most beautiful
words in the English language.
—Henry James

If there were a perfect summer afternoon—
the kind when humidity lowers its head
so day lilies could outsmart the clock
and gladiolas wave to ecstatic birds;
when neighborhood dogs drowse in dreams
of bowls brimmed with nonstop nourishment—
if there were such a day, today is not it.

Nor were all those yesterdays
with the messy beauty of willows,
mimosas, and japonica; with moles
strafing flower beds and raccoons the lawn;
not to mention my inventive escapes
from flamboyant dreams I bet my future on.

Which leads me to this: perfection
is a myth conceived by some
prankster god to uproot tranquility.

So let's dishevel flawlessness and bless
every last-gasp bloom that paid its dues.
Let's praise every weed ignoring
righteous attempts to abort its rebirth.
Let's stand in the middle of the street
and sing—unabashedly off-key—
disco, jazz, folk, soul, and rock.

[. . .]

Or, to temper that thought, let's settle
for declaiming Irving Berlin's love,
blue skies, ragtime, and holidays.
The three-legged tabby with the scruffy coat
and the straying cross-eyed mutt might join in.

To All Dog Owners in the Neighborhood

Enough! The cacophony of barks rolling
from yard to yard is reprehensible
and my only-dogs-can-hear whistle
from Amazon can't silence the din.

You abandon them—chew on that!—
when you're off to work or browsing
in the mall and I'm left with Antonia
howling her anxiety, Beauregard
taunting errant squirrels, and Percy
running amok beneath parked cars.

Don't tell me you love your dog
more than the mother who brushed your hair
or the lover who cuddles you in bed.
And forget the bunk that it's unconditional.
Admit what it is: an addiction
to dopamine from non-judgmental welcomings
every time you mosey through the door.

There must be a 12-step group you could join—
I'll even drive you there—or a therapist
who'll help you fill your dog-size void.
Maybe training in mindfulness?

Yet … I admit when you post videos
of a lab mothering kittens abandoned in a barn
or a mutt pushing a child out of harm's way,
there might be something to this best-friend stuff.

Perhaps I'll buy some Quiet Please Ear Plugs,
turn up my Homedics noise machine,
and re-evaluate. After death I may request
to reincarnate as a non-shedding,
non-yapping, small-pile-pooping pup.
Can you suggest a breed?

Love's Labor's Lost
or Why I Don't Own Pets

Three chameleons
disappeared
into our bamboo shades.
The horny lizard's
soft-curled back
amazed
then,
like goldfish
in their hazy bowl,
flipped
its down side up.
Unamused,
dad booted out
the lab who
slurped
his cabbage soup.
The speckled mutt
arrived
one day,
ran
away the next.
Need more
reasoning?
A droop-face cop
charged
our summer yard
and shot
two frothing pups.

My heart
can't bear
another crack.
I fall in love
too hard,
too fast.

Lament

A modest star
waits in silence
above
a cityscape,
pondering
what might have been
if it were a dandelion,
a hummingbird,
even a fly
scrounging plates
after dinner guests
have gone.

What's the use?
it complains to
a passing cyan gem
when its spurt
of light
leaking through
the random universe
is shunned
by sky glow
and no one
searching
for a dream
thinks
to offer it a wish.

The Fly

I empathize: six days stuck inside our house.
Believe me, I've tried to snatch you in mid-flight
and walk you out the door, but your agility
far out paces mine.

Rest assured, the swatter is in the garage
and, in accordance with my beliefs,
you don't deserve to die. I suspect
you've a mate somewhere who's frantic
for your return and sent out an APB.

This morning you browsed the mail
with special interest in my timeshare's dues—
they're about to rise again—and the pleas
charities send out at least ten times a year.
You also scanned some phrases for poems
I scratched out yesterday.
I couldn't tell if you approved.

Have you noticed we've had frosted nights
and our maples are in autumn bloom?
The slugs have planned their Thanksgiving feast
and juncos and jays are eating seeds
as fast as I can fill their feeders up.

Anyway, before you go—and I hope
you'll find the open window soon—
I want to thank you for motivating me.
After chasing you from room to room
several times a day, I've taken
a mild interest in mild exercise.

To the Spider Clinging to the Windshield of My Honda Fit

What were you thinking?
Even in school zones,
the mph would send
you spinning
into wiper blades
or on to the roof.
This is the last time—
and I mean this emphatically—
I'm pulling into
Safeway's parking lot
or the shoulder of I-205.
Heretofore,
you're on your own.
Don't get me wrong.
I appreciate
the time you take
to tether webs
between our maple trees.
Last week
your sixty-circle trap
bore witness
to patent artistry.
But please be advised:
stay off my Fit
if you want
to weave another day.
And tell your friends
to avoid the space

between cars parked
on our cul-de-sac.
Neighbors intent
on work or groceries
don't appreciate
originality.

Bedeviled

"Giant 'Frog From Hell' Fossil Found in Madagascar"
Brian Handwerk, *National Geographic News*,
February 18, 2008

Scientists have puzzle-pieced fossils
from Africa's southeast and dubbed
their hellish find Beelzebufo.
A crusher of hatchling dinosaurs,
a shredder of lizard skins,
this native South American refined
his Pac Man jaws, buffed up
his steroidal size at every stop
across his continental hop.

I understand his drift.
When human error delays a flight,
I crush coffee cups.
If my seat assignment's lost,
I chew out reservation desks.
Let flight attendants cite the FAA
to tie me to my seat—
it's bathroom or embarrassment—
I puff up into nastiness.

Of all the totems on my pole,
this amphibian is my newest guide.
Let any vertebrate get in my way
or continental drift nudge
me off course, I'll shape-shift.

[. . .]

I won't kill any kid or shred
aging skin, but watch out.
Aggression will ooze
from my furious green eyes.

Eye-Minded

... my poor eyesight makes me see everything in a complete fog.
—Monet

The only thing I hear this summer night
is my rambling mind wondering
how Monet would see my backyard.

If I slip my glasses off, his fog is mine.
Yellow daisies blur behind purple Blazing Stars.
White aster-clusters intertwine.
Hydrangea pinks blemish above a dozen shapes
of shade beneath a smudged maple tree.

Beautiful, Monet would say:
this scene oozing through myopic haze.
I agree. Impressions have their charm.

Yesterday, the doctor said my eyes
are younger than my seventy-six.
Pressure good. Lenses holding strength.
Faint cataracts still faint. And yet ...
what if one day I wake to colors melting
like Monet's? Would I be content to trace
smudges of light reflecting on the backyard pool?
Would I remember the flicker's orange tail,
the bumblebees feasting on lavender?

Since summer is on the run,
I'll put my glasses on and mark memories

like Monet labeled tubes of paint.
I'll even catalog the hostas' late leaf-scorch,
the moss-nibbled edges of lawn,
the ants circling crumbs on the patio.

Variety Is…and 21 Other Proverbs

Variety is the spice, cleanliness is next.

Heaven helps those who don't bite the hand that feeds them.

People who live in glass houses should hope for the best.

There's no place like home for a free lunch.

Necessity makes the heart grow fonder.

A watched pot never spoils the broth.

One man's trash is in the eye of the beholder.

If you can't beat 'em, practice harder.

Honesty is the best policy until it isn't.

You made your bed, now scratch my back.

If you want something done right, lead a horse to water.

Don't cry, don't count: milk and chickens are here today,
    gone tomorrow.

Familiarity breeds the best things in life.

The pen is mightier than a squeaky wheel.

An apple a day is worth a pound of cure.

[. . .]

You have to kiss a lot of toads to starve a fever.

Loose lips make mountains out of molehills.

There are two sides to every story: cross the bridge.

When the going gets tough, make love.

There are two theories about arguing with a woman: try
    putting the cat back in the bag or—the greater part
    of valor—get out of the kitchen.

When all is said and done, what comes around goes.

Quiddity

Maybe it was the writer showing off
her esoteric vocabulary
or the philosopher moping on a park bench,
grasping at the essence of ducks and grass.
Perhaps it arrived in *Word of the Day*
on a day when nothing would quicken
my backyard blooms or stalled poems.

No matter when or where,
quiddity snuck in and nudged me
toward the medieval scribe
in *Merriam-Webster Online*
straining to calligraph *quidditas*
before unbridled dark sabotaged his quill.

As I was typing these words,
that unassuming *q* reminded me
it's the alphabet's seventeenth,
the second most rarely used.

I assured it how bland life would be
without quotidians of quandaries,
quibblings during Q&As,
the quietude of quarks, the quid pro quos
of Quicken and QuickBooks.

I promised to join the blooming Queens—
Lace, Cup, Meadow, Palm, Wreath, and Night—
processing through my neighborhood.

I'll even Google famous names from Qu Yuan
to Quintilian, from Quincy to Star Trek's Q,
and quote them in my epigraphs.
And, in the next life, if children are in the plan,
I'll name a daughter Quinn, a son Quentin.

To: John Q. Poet
From: The IRS
Re: Taxes and Penalties
Date: mm/dd/yyyy

Dear Mr. Poet,

Thank you for your delinquent funds
and the elegiac couplets explaining
their tardiness. I enjoyed *forget/regret*,
taxes/asses set in pentameter, nearly iambic.

As for the penalties, while I understand
you supplement the pennies poets make
with teaching undergrads the rhythmic effects
of dactyls and anapests, my hands are tied.
The rules for fines are as sacred as those
for sonnets, sestinas, and triolets.

With that said, I'd like to share something
you would understand: decades ago
I wrote a poem my high school teacher
penned *Extremely maudlin* in red ink.
I didn't know what *maudlin* meant,
but figured it was not a compliment.
Thanks to her honesty, I spend my days
composing dispassionate retorts
to mawkish letters that grovel and blame.

On a whim, I cc'd your letter upstairs.
Our website editor wants to publish it.

If you approve, send me a third-person bio,
fifty words max. Believe me,
not many are offered this opportunity.

To Capella, the Goat Star

Tonight before I lower my bedroom shades,
I have to tell you there's just no way
I see what astronomers see: a nanny
hanging on the shoulder of a reckless guy
driving a chariot in the western sky
with two kids in the front seat.

Nor can I wrap my mind around your stats:
Twelve times bigger than the Sun.
Surface heat: 4940° Kelvin.
Sixth brightest naked-eye star.
Forty light years away.

I'm more inclined to side with Breton
who calls you "The Shepherd's Star."
1887. Oil on canvas. 40½ by 31.
That's manageable.

I love how you're poised behind
a peasant woman plowing through dusk—
young, barefoot, strong—balancing
an unwieldy sack—potatoes, scholars say—
on the head above her straight-on eyes,
full lips, and determined stride.
Her rustic dress free from dirt and sweat.
Idyllic and romanticized, they say.
Noble in her timelessness.

And there you are: an unassuming light
above impressions of a bare landscape.
The same dazzle I see tonight.

[. . .]

I would like to walk with Breton's girl
and ask about the small scythe in her belt.
I would like to know who's at home
to relieve the weight of work.
Who will rub her feet? Who will offer
a cut of bread, a cup of wine?

Does she appreciate your twinkling steadiness?
Has she wondered, like I do, if you guided
shepherds and kings? If we chatted long enough,
we might agree a practiced fiction becomes belief.

But wait ... the streetlights have hummed on
and the almost-human cries of cats in heat
distract. Since—according to serious gazers
of stars—you never set, hold your answers
for tomorrow night. Shepherd or goat?
Guided or guide? Myth or metaphor?

Replaying the Styx Myth

I never liked it.
Where's the comfort
in a rowboat full
of discontents
who can't agree on
a landing place or price:
the underworld,
Nirvana, heaven,
oblivion?
A coin, enlightenment,
a good life?

I'd rather ride
a life-chasing yacht
and claim the bow—
a Kate
with short hair
shouting to any Leo
who'll hear
I have the currency
to drive
across
wild-waved history.

And when anchored
at my last port-of-call,
I'll sift
through crates
of braided memories
and bless each

misstep, mystery,
victory, loss,
belief, and mis-belief
that forged the first me
into the last.

A Montage of Misperceptions

—after Gerald Stern's " Blue Skies, White Breasts, Green Trees"

1.

What I thought was the unlucky land where clouds end
and eagles crack mountaintops turned out to be
a sunken treasure chest surrounded by a troupe of giggly
goldfish convinced the ocean belongs to them.

2.

What I thought was a bat in my store-bought bag
of spinach, kale, and butter leaf turned out to be
the crumpled title page of *Bel Canto* where someone
wrote "Love and language need not translate."

3.

What I thought was a deluded article—"US Government
claims mermaids do not exist"—turned out to be
a raucous review of *The Sirens' Big Greek Wedding Song,*
a dramady set in Astoria and streamed on Apple TV.

4.

What I thought was a koan about swallowing the Hsi Ch'iang
while floating toward nirvana turned out to be
Balaam's ass strolling down Pennsylvania Avenue,
a delight to biblical scholars who understand irony.

5.

What I thought were black holes devouring cyan gems,
brown dwarfs, and three astrophysicists turned out to be
a rampant case of *metrophobia*—which, I would have staked
my life, meant the dread of cities not the fear of poetry.

Recreating *The Birth of the World*

Joan Miró puzzles me.
A *sort of genesis,* he said, about the surreal world
he brushed, poured, flung unevenly.

In a beginning like his, how do we decide
if he *let there be* a kite or a bird?
Balloons or faceless heads?
A spider stalking a question mark?
Five squiggly lines or horizons, mountains, waves?

Here's my take: Strip the bungling world
of ambiguity and disinvent every living thing—
except for dolphins, giraffes, kittens, pups;
orchards of apple, pear, plum, and hazel nut;
seedling vegetables, a grove of redwood trees.

Then guide it toward the Music of the Spheres
and ask resourceful deities to restyle landscapes
where lions throw complicit nods at antelope,
robins re-gift their vacant nests, and monkeys play
with elephants, rhinos with mountain goats.

And, if they feel magnanimous enough,
creative gods might deign to redesign humanity.
Like surgeons touching babes before they're born,
they could mend the holes in souls before they burst,
eradicate each misshaped truth, convince almost-borns
there'll never be a time they won't exist.

Real or surreal, that's my kind of genesis.

~Addendum~

... In the Drafty Orphanage of a Book
—from Billy Collins, "The Poems of Others"

And that's where they land:

In the top floor dorm,
where an antic ant spouts lines
from *The Rain in Portugal*
and complains about
discarded snips of poetry.
She shares the drafty space
with six stalking ducks,
one sedated frog,
and a grumpy Steller's jay.

On the third grief-filled floor
where mothers/fathers/refugees
hold each other close
and search for comfort hidden
in the dark.

In the second-floor lounge
where Plato, Shakespeare, and Frost
debate eternity with de Chardin,
and Monet swaps perspectives
with Woolf and Thích Nhất Hạnh.

In the first floor's office space,
where a therapist confers with Miró
about poetry's genesis and tenders
advice to distressed retirees.

In the apple-treed backyard,
where Collins bemoans Oliver's demise,
Maggie Smith and Bashō sip mint tea,
Henry James herds flamingoes
and feral cats, and Issa tries
to shush the neighbors' dogs
beneath a budding sky.

After inspecting blueprints,
God is almost content.
He red lines a few mediocre poems
that should be carted off to Goodwill
along with a dozen drafty adjectives.
He orders post-consumer paper—
recycled and acid-free—
to support the renovated edifice.

~Notes~

"Breaking News: God's Rewilding Plan Leaked"

rewilding: returning land to a more natural state

summerize: to prepare a house, car, garden, etc. to counteract the hot weather of summer

"Marx Was Right"

fabulists: my term coined for those who create fables

"Hypnopedia"

Sleep learning

"Reading Billy Collins at 2 A.M."

"The Day Lassie Died" is the name of a Collins poem celebrating this event.

"Dear Type-A Friend"

funemployed: to be without a paying job but enjoying the free time

gadabout: traveling often or to many different places, especially for pleasure

terraform: to alter the environment of a celestial body in order to make it capable of supporting terrestrial life forms

quintillion: a number containing 18 zeros

"To My About-to-Be-Ex Therapist"

ergophobia: an abnormal fear of work or an aversion to work

serigraph: an original silk-screen color print

"Superannuation"

superannuation: retirement, giving up work

nanotechnology: the manipulation of materials on an atomic or molecular scale especially to build microscopic devices

"Music to Disappear By"

Aeolian harp: a stringed musical instrument played by the wind

"What the Recently Dead Are Doing"

bardo: the transitional state between death and rebirth

"Hollow"

This poem is based on a chance encounter on an airplane with a mother who had lost her only son to a rare type of cancer. She was traveling with her husband, two daughters, and a container of the boy's ashes. They indeed took it with them wherever they went, adding travel stickers along the way.

"Anatidaephobia"

anatidaephobia: the irrational fear of being stared at by a duck. The term was coined by Gary Larsen in a Far Side cartoon.

"In Production: *The Flamboyance of Flamingoes*"

ornithologic: a less common term referring to the study of birds

Dictionary.com defined the groups of birds in this poem: a congress of crows, a looming of owls, a kettle of hawks, a conspiracy of ravens, a pitying of doves, a ballet of swans, a flamboyance of flamingoes, a party of peacocks, a waddle of penguins, and a paddling of ducks.

"Blamestorming"

blamestorming: assigning blame to someone or something for an outcome or situation.

"Andragogy 101"

andragogy: theories for how to teach adult learners

"The Best of 42 Writers' Rules for Writing"

These mostly direct quotations are adapted from a list of writers' rules compiled by Emily Harstone in her website Authors Publish.

"Lament"

sky glow: light pollution

"Bedeviled"

bedeviled: to be changed for the worse or to be possessed by a devil

"Eye-Minded"

eye-minded: to be disposed to perceive one's environment in visual terms and to recall sights more vividly than sounds, smells, or touch

"Quiddity"

quiddity: the essence of a thing

"To: John Q. Poet…"

maudlin: overly sentimental. On a personal note, my high school English teacher wrote "extremely maudlin" on the one and only poem I wrote as a senior. It's amazing I've continued to write.

"A Montage of Misperceptions"

metrophobia: the irrational fear of poetry

~Acknowledgments~

Many thanks to the editors of these publications for believing in these poems. Some have appeared in these journals or anthologies in slightly different versions and with different titles.

Abstract Magazine: Contemporary Expressions, "Marx Was Right"

Amethyst Review, "About Nothing"

Ample Remains, "It Was a Dark and Rainy Night at the Poetry Salon"

Change Seven, "What the Recently Dead Are Doing"

Dime Show Review, "The Fly"

Dissonance, "Partners of Poets Anonymous (POPA) Opening for Business"

Gyroscope Review, "In Production: *The Flamboyance of Flamingoes*"

Hive Avenue Literary Review, "Bedeviled," "To: John Q. Poet"

Jam and Sand, "Superannuation," "Dear Type-A Friend"

MORIA, "The Best of 42 Writers' Rules for Writing"

Naugatuck River Review, "Music to Disappear By"

Not Very Quiet, "Blamestorming"

pãn/dé/mik: An Anthology of Pandemic Poetry, "Contemplating Distancing"

Postcard Poems and Prose Magazine, "A Week Late"

QU, Queens University of Charlotte, NC, "Anatidaephobia"

Rat's Ass Review, "*Everything That Rises Must Converge*," "*Variety Is*...and 21 Other Proverbs"

Redheaded Stepchild, "Hypnopedia"

San Antonio Review, "To All the Dog Owners in the Neighborhood," "Twenty-One Epigraphs for Poems Celebrating the Retirement of Work Addicts"

Smitten: This Is What Love Looks Like, "Just Saying"

Snapdragon: A Journal of Art and Healing, "Eye-Minded"

Soul-Lit, "Lament"

Stonecrop Magazine, "After Reading Khaled Housseini's *Sea Prayer*"

The Blue Nib, "Dear Billy Collins," "In Praise of Community," "Pay Attention and You're Saved," "To My About-to-Be-Ex Therapist"

The Ekprastic Review, "To Capella, the Goat Star"

The Magnolia Review, "From Your Resident Steller's Jay," "Playing Second Violin," "Replaying the Styx Myth"

The Poeming Pigeon: Cosmos, "In Praise of Errancy," "Recreating *The Birth of the World*"

The Sandy River Review, "To the Young Couple I Embarrassed on the Train while Riding Home from the Airport after a Trip to Rocky Mountain National Park"

The Writers and Readers Magazine, "A Sonnet to Early Spring," "Because the Sky," "*Don't Follow a Good Dead Poet, but Search for What He Searched for*," "Time Management in Grand Central Bakery"

Unearthed, "Breaking News: God's Rewilding Plan Leaked"

VoiceCatcher, "Apologies to Mary Oliver," "To the Spider
Clinging to the Windshield of My Honda Fit"

Willawaw Journal, "Mosaic of a Spring Day in Quarantine"

Writing in a Woman's Voice, "Hollow"

Yellow Arrow Journal, "Mandate"

Zingara Poetry Review, "Tethering"

~Praise for *The Catolog of Small Contentments*~

Fast-paced and quick-witted, Carolyn Martin's fifth collection, *The Catalog of Small Contentments*, will lift your spirits, entertain and fortify you during these mad times. These are love songs to the world and all that lives within it. There are laugh-out loud poems and poems of praise to the maker of the universe, to the earth in all its beauty. Find here ekphrastic poems that reconsider surrealism and poetry, turning old myths into new understandings. John Donne's *For God's sake, hold your tongue and let me love* and Noel Coward's *Kiss me quick before my body rots* set the tone for a collection that takes its own advice to poets: *Never ride a bike with the brakes on*. Philosophical and funny, wise and rhythmic, Martin's exuberance for living will infect and sustain every reader.

—Felicia McCarthy,
The Blue Nib's Poetry Editor for North American Time,
author of *The Gypsy Shaman's Daughter*

Small contentments appear throughout Carolyn Martin's fifth poetry collection with an abundance of gratitude. One can feel the natural world of human and animal life— in heart, in mind, in ocean, in garden— speaking out from deep inside the poet.

The humility that gratitude requires also shines in these poems alongside Martin's compelling impatience for the suffering that diminishes us. Her quiet anger flows through poems like "Breaking News: God's Rewilding Plan Leaked" where human inattention and grandiosity undermine some of the awesome contentments that the world can provide. Humans might

[. . .]

well be in Martin's thoughts when she writes in "A Montage of Misperceptions," *giggly goldfish [are] convinced the ocean belongs to them.*

The Catalog of Small Contentments reads like an injection of the human spirit into the bloodstream.

—Colin Greer, poet, playwright, educator, activist, and president of The New World Foundation

Carolyn Martin's *The Catalog of Small Contentments* suggests how we can find sanity in what we see in our gardens, poetry books, or the night school of sleeplessness and dreams. Whatever is close by, including feral cats. She notices the spider on her windshield and writes with a robust sense of humor which hits perfect notes in her laugh-out-loud proverbs. Her serious side pays homage to influences as diverse as Billy Collins, Bashō, Marx, and Bette Davis. We witness her gentle compassion when she reads obituaries and shares the loss of loved ones. Martin's fans might include other poets, mystics, birdwatchers, retired folks, and those open to learning a new word a day (she provides an addendum to explain.) Boiling it down, these poems are for people who wonder about the place of humans in the universe on days that begin with a look out the window.

—Tricia Knoll, author of *Checkered Mates*

~About the Author~

From associate professor of English to management trainer to retiree, Carolyn Martin has journeyed from New Jersey to Oregon to discover Douglas firs, months of rain, and dry summers. After years of writing academic papers and business books, she discovered that poetry is the way her mind interacts with the world—in images, rhythms, sounds, and intensities of language. So she's settled into the joyful challenge of translating experience into as few words as possible and making those experiences accessible to her readers.

Martin prides herself on flashes of humor that light up her poems. Her intention is to begin and end poems with delight and throw in splashes of wisdom along the way. Add her penchant for musicality and obsession with unusual words, she crafts poems that are surprising and satisfying.

Her poems have appeared in more than 130 journals and anthologies throughout North America, Australia, and the UK. Her fourth poetry collection, *A Penchant for Masquerades*, was released by Unsolicited Press in 2019, and her first chapbook, *Nothing More to Lose*, by The Poetry Box in 2020.

She currently serves as poetry editor of *Kosmos Quarterly: journal for global transformation*.

<carolynmartinpoet.com>

~About The Poetry Box~

The Poetry Box® is a boutique publishing company in Portland, Oregon, which provides a platform for both established and emerging poets to share their words with the world through beautiful printed books and chapbooks.

Feel free to visit the online bookstore (thePoetryBox.com), where you'll find more titles including:

Nothing More to Lose by Carolyn Martin

The Way A Woman Knows by Carolyn Martin

Broadfork Farm by Tricia Knoll

Like the O in Hope by Jeanne Julian

A Shape of Sky by Cathy Cain

The Very Rich Hours by Gregory Loselle

Shadow Man by Margaret Chula

Between States of Matter by Sherry Rind

Sophia & Mister Walter Whitman by Penelope Scambly Schott

A Long, Wide Stretch of Calm by Melanie Green

The Kingdom of Birds by Joan Colby

and more . . .